By Laura Williams
Translated by Zainab Shah

1 rue de l'église, 91430 Igny
Dépôt légal : Décembre 2022
ISBN 978-2-494614-60-4
Imprimé à la demande par Amazon
Loi n° 49-956 du 16 juillet 1949 sur les publications destinées à la jeunesse

سونا

[sona] - to sleep

نهانا

[nahana] - to take a bath

رینگنا

[reengna] - to crawl

كهيلنا

[khailna] - to play

بیٹھنا

[baithna] - to sit

رونا

[rona] - to cry

کھڑا ہونا

[khara houna] - to stand

تالی بجانا

[taali bajana] - to clap

پڑھنا

[parhna] - to read

كهانا

[khaana] - to eat

پینا

[peena] - to drink

ہنسنا

[hansna] - to laugh

گلے لگانا

[galay lagana] - to hug

چلنا

[chalna] - to walk

دوڑنا

[dourna] - to run

چومنا

[chumna] - to kiss

کودنا

[kudna] - to jump

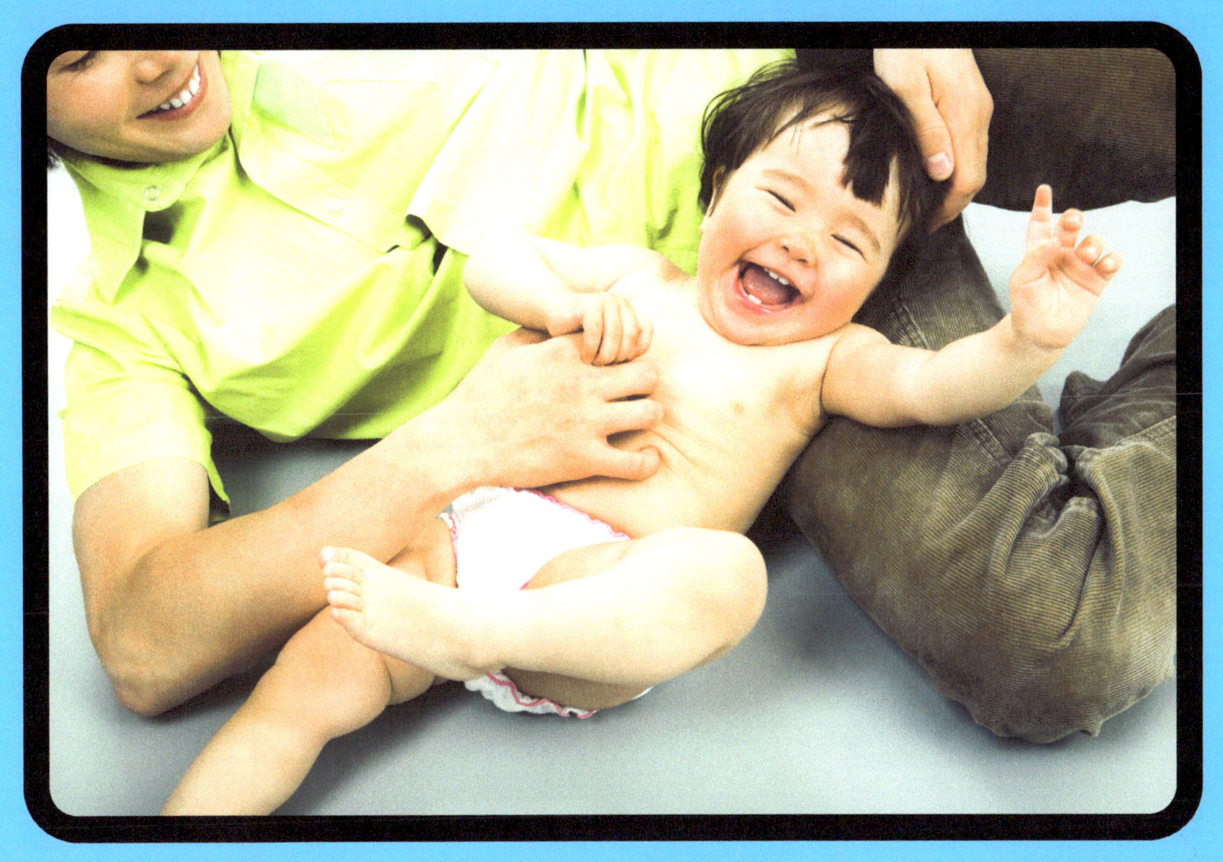

گدگدی کرنا

[gudgudi karna] - to tickle

ناچنا

[nachna] - to dance

پکانا

[pakana] - to cook

گھٹنے ٹیکنا

[ghutnay taikna] – to kneel

دهكيلنا

[dhakelna] - to push

کھینچنا

[khainchna] - to pull

لکھنا

[likhna] - to write

گانا

[gana] - to sing

Thank you

Thank you for purchasing "Urdu-English Words for Toddlers"! Your support means a lot to me, and I hope you and your child enjoy these books.

If you have a moment, I would greatly appreciate it if you could leave a review on Amazon. Your feedback will help me improve future editions of the series and create more resources for bilingual children.

Thank you again for your support. You can access the reviews on Amazon by scanning the QR code below or by visiting the link below:

https://www.amazon.com/review/create-review?&asin=2494614600

Thank you for helping me continue my work as a language teacher and translator. Your support is greatly appreciated!

In the same collection

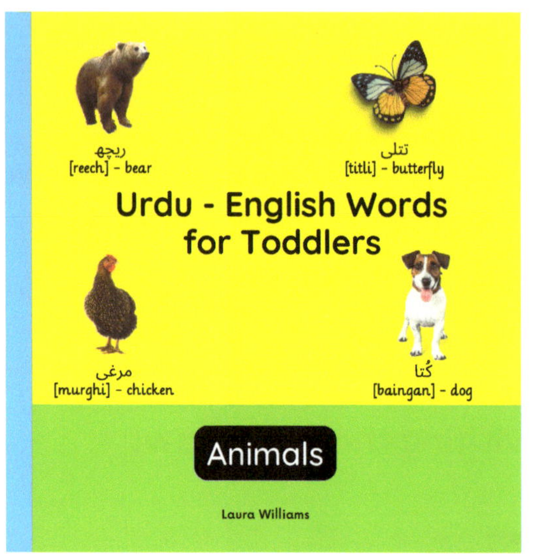

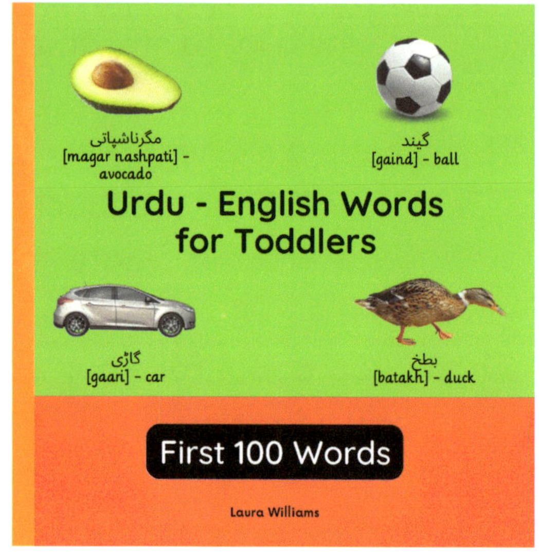

www.ingramcontent.com/pod-product-compliance
Lightning Source LLC
LaVergne TN
LVHW071232160826
845679LV00003B/966
* 9 7 8 2 4 9 4 6 1 4 6 0 4 *